ACKNOWL[

I would love to express my gratitude to Book Leaf publishing for giving me this amazing opportunity which has also helped me grow as a person.

I would not have been able to write such things without going through the things I have in my life and knowing people that have also gone through hard times. And for that I have to thank everyone that ever hurt me and ever told me I couldn't when I could. You helped me write a book.

I could not be where I am today if it weren't for the people I surround myself with. I do not wish to name these people as they change all the time, but they know who they are and they know how much I appreciate them. However one person I will name is my son. He gives me strength, he takes it away too of course but he always returns it with a smile and a giggle and I would not be the person I am today if I didn't have him.

And lastly I would like to thank Helen Keller. Even though I do not know her she provided a quote which I live my life by. "The best and most beautiful things in the world cannot be seen or even touched they must be felt with the heart".

PREFACE

I want to share my experiences and things that I have learnt in a beautiful way. A lot of the things I write about are things that have happened to me or around me, however other things I just know about and don't feel that they are talked about enough. Poetry is always something that has flowed through me as I am a musician, and I believe that lyrics are just poems set to music. Since secondary school I have wanted to write poems and have my work published, and through school competitions I have; however I was doing things like that for the wrong reasons, but this; this is for all the right reasons.

Hands

Hands were made for holding
To use when embracing
Showing signs of affection

But you showed me gripping
And ploughing with your fingers
Not the kind I was taught to expect

Your grip got tighter
Your fingers ploughed deeper
Harder
Faster

I lay there trying to force out a moan
Like they do in the 'movies'
You always said I was a good actor

I Love You

We are made to believe
That the words I Love You
Mean less and less,
The more partners you say it to
That it loses its sincerity
I have told many partners these words
It's meaning grew overtime
For It is only now that I realise
What those words truly mean

Scars and Tattoos

I have only one tattoo
And more scars than I can count
From falling off bikes
Or picking at scabs
But each one of your words
Scars my brain
Each of your actions
Tattoos my self worth
Maybe if I am lucky
They will fade over time
And I will once again
Be strong

Two Meals A Day

I saw a post online from a woman who had lost
weight. She said how happy she was and how
unhealthy it is to eat more than two meals a day.
If you snack, stop, she said. It's why you're fat
or overweight. Two meals a day. She had lost so
much weight.

When thin people get thinner they are sick and
need help. When a bigger person gets thinner,
they are a marvel, a topic of conversation. Look
at you finally taking care of yourself. I am so
proud of you. What's the secret.

Because I was not thin I am not sick. I am an
icon. Everyone wants to know my secret. How
did you lose so much so fast? I haven't eaten in
4 days, they laugh like I am joking when inside I
am dying. Dying to be thinner, dying to feel
pretty, dying to like myself and dying so they
like me too.

But because I was not thin to begin with I am
not sick. I am taking care of myself.

If only they knew how wrong they are.

Old Fashioned

Old Fashioned

In this day and age full of technology and
deception
All most of us want is a old fashioned kind of
love.
A love that doesn't need a text or a phone call to
survive
But an I love you or that dimple in your smile.
I've studied your face and every line in your
hand
As If I were studying for an exam and the topic
is you.
But really all it is that I am studying for
Is our life and our future we are beginning to
explore.

Cut

I wish I could cut people out of my life
As easily as I cut paper
I could shut people out
Pretend they do not exist
I cannot do this
I am always attached
I do not know why I cannot do it
Why I am always attached
I know it is unhealthy
Yet for some reason I cannot stop

Scent

Your body is like a drug
Your scent lingers on the sheets
And when you are away
I want it all over me

Long Distance

From a thousand miles away, I can feel your breath by my ear
Whispering I love you, loud and clear
You do not have to be beside me for your presence to linger on
But I suppose I should stop with this star I'm wishing on
It's not that you moved away or moved on with your life
But that you moved away with someone else, ready to make her your wife
You always said you would never get married, not ever, not at all
But when you popped her the question, I've never felt so small
Like a grain of sand on a child's dirty hand
Sitting among others, looking for a soft place to land
Long distance is always hard, but they never said it would be this way
When the one you long for, is with someone else, and a thousand miles away.

Small

There is a tiny me in my head, sitting in the
middle of my brain
Who goes over all my decisions, and decides
what I do and don't say
Sometimes, when the world gets on top of me,
and all my emotions become heavy
She gets smaller, and smaller, until she is hardly
there at all
Sand bags sit on top of her, labelled with
different things
Like depression, classwork, body image, and
other words that sting
There's times when she gets big again, and she
feels really good
But it takes a small inconvenience to make her
feel just like she did before
Irritating, unimportant, but most of all

small

Girl Code

there is girl code and guy code and everything in
between
but what if the person you want, pretends you
aren't seen
ignores you every day, acts like you don't exist
because in they're world, you aren't important
enough to be noticed
they're the main character, and you aren't even a
best friend, a lover, or an enemy

you're just in the background

Everywhere

It's hard to describe you, when I see you in all
that I do
In every cup of tea, in every droplet covered
window
I can't talk about you without seeing your face,
everywhere
I can't concentrate, I can't see straight, I can't
focus on anything
Because everything reminds me of you
I see you everywhere

I have never envied the blind, so fucking much

Old Flame

We all love an old flame really, don't we.
Weather it be an ex of some kind, or someone
that once could have been something,
Or maybe a visit home, and you lock eyes with
your old flame in a supermarket isle
Picking out which tub of strawberries you're
going to have with your ice cream.
Maybe it's a location
A place you always used to go
"That's our spot" you used to say.
"That's where we first kissed"
"That's where I cut my hand on a broken bottle
after you threw it in the water"
We don't forget our old flames, they are
memories, pieces of us
People we won't soon forget
Places we no longer visit in person, but often in
dreams
Foods we no longer eat
Shoes we no longer wear
A hand we no longer hold
When a person, a place, a food, a shoe, or a
hand, are no longer what they used to be
Now they are only an old flame

Tsunami

Tsunami- an arrival or occurrence of something
in overwhelming quantities or amounts

How about that, overwhelming is the key word
there for me
How can a tsunami of thoughts about you flood
my mind so easily?
Overwhelming
Your deceit and your lies always plagued me and
puts gasoline on my fire
The fire that burns inside me at the mention of
your name, making the flames grow higher and
higher.
The shivers that overcome my body at the sight
of you
The things I hate to think but nevertheless I still
do
How you caressed every inch of my skin
Then I remember the look on your face when I
walked in
How her skin must have felt, beneath your
fingertips
How her pink lipstick, was all over your lips
I wonder if it still is, or if she wasn't worth the
hassle

Now you're not around, I'm the queen of my
own castle
I don't need a Prince, in fact I never did
Thoughts of only relief come now, when the
tsunami hits

Stargazing

Big flaming balls of gas a million miles away,
"The stars you're seeing, are already dead" is
what they always say.
I don't believe that, I think they live forever,
Just like that feeling we both had, when we went
stargazing together.
There's so many constellations, so many stories
written in the sky,
Being tormented by something so beautiful,
knowing it has to die.
Laid on that field there with you, feeling like I
could stay there forever,
And other blissful things that I thought, when we
went stargazing together.

Getting Lost

When the world gets too loud and I find it hard
to breathe
I go to my favourite place, a book I like to read.
Maybe something like The Great Gatsby, or If I
Stay,
All I know is in my books, I can always run
away.
No consequences, no mothers saying no,
Only a heart full of wonder, and a main
character saying "go".
The pages are full of wisdom, and boys I wish I
could date in real life,
Animals that talk and magical kingdoms filled
with strife.
I can always come back, whenever I want,
We can all do, with a bit of getting lost.

7 Days

On Monday, you told me you loved me, and
kissed me goodnight.
On Tuesday, I asked who she was and we got in
a fight.
On Wednesday, you were distant, cold.
On Thursday, your face was a sight to behold.
On Friday, you screamed at me and called me
every name under the sun.
On Saturday, I told you I'd had enough and I was
done.
On Sunday, I saw you out, with her, she has your
heart.

On Monday, I felt as though my soul had been
torn apart.

The Bystander Effect

We all people watch from time to time no matter
how much we deny it
We don't even realise most of the time what
we're doing, not even a little bit.
We gaze out of windows to pass the time
And watch other's conversations, unfold before
our eyes.
The rolling of eyes, the biting of lips
When a passer-by sniggers, as someone else
trips.
The morbid curiosity to revel in other peoples
suffering, as long as its not our own
Interested in all the people we pass on our way
home.
We feel the need to tell someone, the secrets we
overhear
And we slightly break inside, when we hear
something we fear.
A relative is sick, that man's son didn't get into
university,
The woman down the road, her cat died, oh my,
what a pity.
We all people watch you see, we are bystanders
in the experiment that is society,
Weather its watching someone propose, or
hearing someone broke sobriety.

We stand, we sit, we watch, we stand by,
Waiting to see something that sends our plans
awry.

The Tree

We all have somewhere we go to, to calm
ourselves down
To talk to a loved one we have lost, to confess
our plans to paint the town
For me It's always a tree, I find one everywhere I
move to
It sounds bizarre I know, but there's just
something about them I love
As if something bigger is calling me, something
from above
I climb them and sit on the largest branch I can
find
I often give them names, I remember each one
left behind
I grow up, I move on, I find a new tree
But I could never forget the ones that were
always there for me
When my granddad passed, and I needed to cry
it out
When a friend betrayed me and I needed to
scream and shout
My trees were always there for me, what about
you, what's yours?
The place you go to, despite all it's flaws
My trees often had bugs, and bird poo I'd
accidentally sit on

Maybe you have a chair, or a bench you perch
upon
Either way, no matter where it is
Don't lose it or forget it, It'll always be your one
true bliss.

Touch

When did fingertips become the cause for
shivers down my spine
When did eye contact mean something else
entirely
When did a raised hand for a high five mean I
had to cower
When did a crooked smile mean I was in trouble
Ever since You.
You took way my innocence and everything I
used to love
You ripped the pages out of my favourite book,
now I can't pick it up
You laughed at my troubles, they were a joke
and so was I
You clipped my wings
But now without you
I can fly

Ingram Content Group UK Ltd.
Milton Keynes UK
UKHW020632310323
419456UK00014B/761